T0365372

THE VIEW FROM POVERTY RIDGE

a collection of essays and photographs by
Joseph F. Persinger

Book Designer: Jonah Goodman
Art Director: Mike Nardone

To order additional copies of this book, contact:
Xlibris
844-714-8691
www.Xlibris.com
Orders@Xlibris.com

ISBN: Softcover   978-1-4010-8675-6

Library of Congress Control Number: 2002096552

Print information available on the last page

Rev. date: 04/20/2021

INTRODUCTION

When Indiana photojournalist Joseph F. Persinger and his wife, Judy, sold their house in town and moved into a small cabin in a rural neighborhood known as "Poverty Ridge," he decided to chronicle their experiences in a series of columns entitled "The View from Poverty Ridge," referring to the view of the countryside from their new location as well as the editorial views of the author.

Combining humor, pathos, and nostalgia, the series attracted a loyal following of readers and was honored by the Hoosier State Press Association as "Best General Column" in its Better Newspaper Contest. Judges of that event described Persinger's essays as "well written and interesting . .. Good grasp of small town America . . . Persinger tells the stories in his column very well, even sharing a lesson or two along the way . . . Persinger is not the 'grouchiest old coot in Indiana' and seeing through his facade is half the fun of reading his columns."

This collection features 28 of those essays and 22 of Persinger's scenic photographs.

We've Gone Country . . . But Why?

We spent such a long time looking for a place in the country that by the time we found our spot here in the Poverty Ridge area I'd almost forgotten what motivated us. A couple of weeks ago, something happened to remind me.

In the last three or four years we had looked at dozens of pieces of property. Most of them had some drawback that was obvious as soon as you drove up. Others were pretty good, and a couple were so attractive that we made formal offers on them, but for various reasons they didn't work out. When we finally came upon our present location, we figured the reason those other deals fell through was that this is where we were meant to be. We still feel that way.

But during all that looking the search became almost an end in itself, and the reasons faded into the background. It took a freak of nature to bring things back into focus.

One afternoon we actually managed to get away from the office at five o'clock sharp and hurried home while it was still daylight. I quickly changed into my work clothes, fired up the old Wheel Horse lawn tractor and headed out to the top of one of the ridges near the county road. There's a knoll there that has a decent-sized flat area at the top before it slopes off, abruptly, toward the little pond. I wanted to mow that flat area just to clean it up a little with an eye toward planting some grapevines there later this spring.

From the top of that hill, you look toward the south and southwest. At the bottom of the hill the little pond was reflecting the sky. The sky itself was looking kind of threatening. There were big clumps of very dark blue — almost black — clouds gathering right in front of the late afternoon sun. Here and there the sun broke through the clouds in hazy shafts of golden light. It was the kind of sky that always makes me think of those old Charlton Heston epic movies, right at the point where the narrator says: "And the Lord spoke unto Moses . . . ."

No one spoke, but a few raindrops fell, and I began to wonder if I would get to finish my mowing. But the rain soon stopped, and I continued to zoom around on my Wheel Horse in gradually decreasing circles. Then the bizarre part happened.

It started to hail. Hailstones about the size of the tip of my little finger began to fall all around, coming down faster and faster, bouncing off the grass. They didn't hurt; they weren't real hard — kind of slushy and yet still distinctly rounded.

Then, as the hailstorm continued, the clouds moved a little more to the east, revealing the sun. What a color picture it would have made: the sun shining brightly while the hailstones peppered down onto the greening grass all around a man on a bright red lawn tractor driving around and around on top of the little hill with the storm clouds still reflecting brilliantly on the surface of the pond below. Then — and I'm not making this up — a single Canada goose came flying over and, for a few brief seconds, became a part of the scene.

Of course, I didn't have my camera with me. And if I did have a picture of it, people would probably think it wasn't real. The colors were too bright and gaudy, there were too many things going on — too many elements for one picture. It would have looked like one of those garish composite pictures advertising people create on computers.

But it was real, and for about 30 seconds it was truly breath-taking. And it reminded me why I had been longing to get back to the country.

It reminded me of times, as a boy, when I would come upon a sunset — the sky all red and lavender over the peaks of the dark dusty blue-gray hills southeast of town — and my little heart would just about burst with joy at the sight of something so magnificent. And then would come a twinge of sadness because there was no way to capture the beauty of it and share it with Mimi and Grandpa or Mom and Dad.

Maybe that's why I became a photographer. It's definitely why I wanted to get back to the country. Now I remember . . . .

A Time to Till, To Sow, To Leap

When my wife and I moved to a small house in the country we knew that, come spring, we would have to create some additional living space. We approached the construction project with some apprehension, having heard numerous horror stories from friends about their house-building experiences. Fortunately, we were only adding a family room, screened-in porch, and a deck — not building an entire house.

The project went smoothly, thanks to the contractors who were extremely patient and didn't seem to mind taking time to explain when we asked silly questions about what they were doing.

The only thing that required much effort on our part was helping coordinate various aspects of the project. For example, the heating and air conditioning workers had to do their installation at just the right point in the general construction so the project could move forward. Then we had to coordinate the schedules of the bulldozer man, who had to reshape the hillsides around the house, and the gas company servicemen who had to relocate the big liquid propane gas tank and run a new gas line.

The first day the bulldozer man came he smoothed out the slope on the north side of the house. Then, the next morning, the gas company workers came and moved the LP tank from the south side of the house to the north side, up by the barn. They ran a new copper line underground from the tank down the newly worked slope to the house. Then, with the tank out of the way, the bulldozer man could finish his work on the south side.

At that point, although construction was virtually completed, we now had freshly worked soil, instead of grass, on both sides of the house. And then it rained, and we had mud. When we left for work in the morning we had to carry our good shoes and wear some old boots to get from the house to the car.

We needed to get some grass started, so as soon as the soil dried enough to work, I borrowed a rear-tine tiller from a neighbor, bought a huge bag of grass seed and several bales of straw, and went to work. Coming home on a Wednesday afternoon, I toiled furiously in the hot sun, trying to get the front section tilled, seeded, rolled, and strawed because it was supposed to rain again that night (and it did).

Back and forth I went, strolling along behind the tiller on the down slope and huffing, puffing, and grunting in the 90-degree heat as I shoved the tiller back up the incline. Now, keep in mind that this was on the north side of the house.

Having worked about halfway through the area, I was wrestling the tiller through the heavy clay when it suddenly bucked and jumped violently, and the handles were almost torn from my hands. At the same time I heard a loud hissing sound, and immediately I knew what had happened — I had tilled right through the new gas line.

Fearing any second I might be blown to kingdom come, I turned to head for the shut-off valve on the gas tank 50 feet away while simultaneously jerking back on the throttle of the tiller to turn off the engine. My back was already turned to the tiller at that point, my hand leaving the throttle, when the tiller, having been shut off so abruptly — backfired.

Ka-Bam!

Long jump was not my chosen event in high school track, but had I been able to duplicate the leap I made that afternoon, I could have won the state title with ease. But with the gas valve turned off, and realizing that nothing had exploded, my pulse began to return to normal, and panic gave way to mumbling and grumbling.

My wife had pulled up in the car just as all this was taking place, and was standing there watching my antics with an amazed expression.

Knowing I would not relish the thought of having to call the gas company and tell them what happened, she volunteered to do it for me. And, to their credit, when the workers came out the next day to run the new gas line — again — they worked in silence, offering no editorial comments about the inadvisability of turning certain people lose with power tillers.

Their restraint was certainly appreciated.

SPRING CREEK

10 Acres and a Calico Cat

We didn't have any pets when we moved out here to Poverty Ridge. It turned out that was a good thing, since a cat came with the place. It's a calico cat — splotchy orange and black and white — with some poorly placed black spots on a face that, frankly, is not very attractive. It's an ugly cat (although my wife, Judy, doesn't like for me to say that — especially if the cat is close enough to hear me). So far it has no name. We just refer to it as "Kitty" or "Cat." Not very imaginative, but the perfect name just hasn't suggested itself.

We don't know where this cat came from. It may have belonged to the former owner of the property or, for all we know, it may belong to a neighbor and is just coming over to our place to mooch some food, but it seems to be here most of the time. It's at the back door waiting to be fed every morning, and it's usually at the front door waiting for us when we get home at night. It frequently brings mice and chipmunks it has caught and places them on the porch for our approval. These little gifts do not make a great impression on Judy, however.

We're not really interested in having an "inside cat," but that doesn't stop it from trying to slip into the house at every opportunity. If it gets in, it darts under the bed, where it is next to impossible to catch. But eventually it ventures out into the kitchen and begins exploring in the vicinity of the tin canister where we keep the cat food, which gives us a chance to catch it and put it back outside. Its food dish and water dish are on the porch, and there's a nice dry barn with a bed of straw where the cat can find shelter from the elements.

The odd thing is that this cat, despite its obvious desire to be near us, is not very affectionate. It does not like to be held and within 15 seconds of being picked up will begin to struggle furiously to get down. But if you're sitting on the porch, it will rub against your legs and purr.

One afternoon after doing some outdoor work, I sat down in a lawn chair and lifted the cat onto my lap. Instead of trying to hold it, I just let the cat sit there on its own. This time it didn't seem so anxious to get down, but as it sat there and started to purr it also began flexing its long, sharp claws in a kind of pulsating rhythm, sinking them deeper and deeper into my thigh, prompting me to end that "bonding" session.

Still, it's interesting the way we respond to animals — to their distinctive personalities — and it will be interesting to see what kind of relationship eventually develops between us and the no-name cat. Perhaps it will turn out to be one of those memorable pets that is like a member of the family, complete with its own collection of cute stories: Remember when the cat used to zoom into the house and hide under the bed?

Maybe it's starting already, but only time will tell.

I come to the
Garden alone
While the dew
Is still —

A Most Memorable Role

I enjoy Father's Day more now than I did when my kids were little. Oh, it was fun then, too, of course, but a lot noisier. And the kids, too young to really understand, were just following Mom's instructions when they made cards or gifts or tried to prepare a special meal.

Now when they come by the house, as young adults, it seems to have more meaning. Sunday afternoon we sat and talked; they filled us in on their jobs and/or college classwork, and we recalled a few happy memories from the past. The grandkids livened things up for a while as they attacked the angel food cake and strawberries, but for the most part it was a quiet, reflective kind of day.

As a slightly deranged individual whose life has been loosely based on the movies he has seen, I couldn't help thinking about "The Godfather" as the stream of cars approached throughout the afternoon, bringing children, stepchildren, and grandchildren to pay respect to the old man.

I had to resist the urge to stuff my cheeks with Kleenex and do my best Marlon Brando impression: "Someday, and that day may never come, I will ask you to do a service for me . . . ."

And I think my recent appearance as 80-year-old Norman Thayer in the community theatre production of "On Golden Pond" had an impact on both me and the kids. For better or worse, we all got a glimpse of the future.

While we were working on that play, the director, Dr. Joel McGill, pointed out that part of Norman's abrasive personality could have been the result of a fairly common medical phenomenon in which older people lose their inhibitions about saying certain things. They make comments that seem tactless or even hurtful, but they don't have any sense of being unkind — they're just saying what they think. It reminded me of a quotation attributed to former President Harry S. Truman. "I don't give 'em hell," Truman told a reporter. "I just tell the truth, and they think it's hell."

Anyway, growing older doesn't seem like such a terrible thing now after spending that time as Norman and having such a pleasant time Sunday fulfilling my real life role as Dad and Grandpa.

Speaking of inhibitions, a lot of us come from families where feelings were not readily expressed. Rev. Ewick spoke about that in his sermon Sunday morning at the Methodist Church, sharing a personal experience that brought a tear to everyone's eyes as he told how his father, with virtually his last breath, pulled him close and whispered — for the first, only, and last time — "I love you, Carl."

But, although we may not have said, "I love you" frequently, our fathers knew we loved them, and we certainly knew they loved us.

For whatever reason, young people today have escaped that inhibition, and it's a wonderful thing. And because they're not afraid to say "I love you," they've helped us older folks become more comfortable with expressing our feelings too.

Maybe that's the best Father's Day gift of all.

BUTTERFLY BUSH VISITOR

LESSONS FROM THE BERRY PATCH

I did something the other day I hadn't done for a long time — nothing stupendous, I just picked a little pailful of blackberries — enough for Judy to make a couple of pies.

We noticed when we moved out here to the ridge that there were several wild blackberry patches around the property, but in the years since then the berries have been hard, nubby little things that seemed to turn from green to red and then just disappear. This year, though, the briars are loaded with plump berries that are now rapidly turning from red to glossy black.

Blackberries have a flavor that is unique — a deep, dark, winey taste unlike any other fruit. Kids like them, of course, but I like to think that blackberries are really intended for adults. The ritual of getting ready to go to the berry patch, followed by the actual foray into the tangled, thorny thicket brought back a lot of memories.

As a youngster I spent most of my summer days at my grandparents' home which, fortunately, was located less than a hundred yards up the hill behind my parents' house. My grandparents' property had both black raspberry and blackberry patches. In June we would pick raspberries from tall, greenish-white brambles that grew in a thicket just west and north of the outhouse and along the western edge of the garden. Blackberries could be found in various locations scattered around the property, and they were picked around the Fourth of July.

Before going out to the berry patch, the sensible picker would dress in a long-sleeved shirt, long pants, and a hat — in part as a shield against the sun and the brambles and in part for protection from the dreaded chigger and the nefarious tick.

In those days we had never heard of commercial insect repellent, but my grandparents had their own recipe. Just before heading out the door, they would take small strips of cloth torn from an old sheet or pillowcase and dip them in kerosene. (My grandmother cooked on a wood-fired cook stove in the winter and on a kerosene stove during the summer, so they always had a can of kerosene around). They would tie the petroleum-dampened cloth around their shirt cuffs at the wrist and their pants cuffs at the ankle as an additional protection against vampire insects. With all those preparations completed, you were finally ready to pick some berries.

I quickly discovered I had forgotten some of the less romantic aspects of berry picking as I struggled to get a foothold on the dew-slick grass and weeds, slipping on decaying tree limbs that lay hidden beneath the undergrowth as the July sun beat down and sweat trickled into my eyes, a persistent mosquito made zing-singing orbits around my ears, and the thorns left bloody little itching scratches on the backs of my hands.

But those things were quickly forgotten later in the day as Judy scooped a big wedge of blackberry pie onto my plate.

It occurred to me that our best memories seldom arise from moments of unchallenged bliss but from the happiness that follows when we push on to reach our goal undeterred by temporary discomfort, fear, or danger — even in such small things as berry picking. I doubt that many young people today are motivated to plunge into the thickets in search of berries. And that's too bad.

DAYLILY AND BERRIES

Some Things Are Best Forgotten

How is it that wives and husbands ever manage to get along? They are such totally different creatures, moving through this world on entirely separate planes.

Generally speaking, wives are attuned to the small details while husbands see only "the big picture." Wives think long and hard about things that never cross the mind of a husband — things like color-coordinated bedsheets, clean bathrooms, or remembering birthdays and anniversaries.

And wives possess some extraordinary abilities, including a kind of psychic power that allows them to see through walls and read minds. Without giving any clue as to where I am headed or why, I can leave the family room, go into the kitchen, quietly open the cupboard and stare at its contents for maybe five seconds before Judy calls from the other room: "It's on the bottom shelf, on the left!"

Knowing there is no way she can possibly know what I am looking for, I ask: "What is?"

"The new jar of salsa," she replies, correctly.

How do they do that?

Wives never forget. A wife can remember every detail of an outfit she wore to a New Year's Eve party in 1964. A husband can't remember what he wore yesterday. And that unshakable memory is not limited to clothing.

Let's take a purely hypothetical situation: Suppose a husband goes outside on an early spring day to do some yard work. He notices that, during the winter, lots of dead leaves and other debris have collected in the bottom foot or so of the tall hedge that provides a screen along one side of the back yard patio. The hedge is still dormant, and the accumulated organic matter is well below the leafy area of the hedge. He tries using a leaf rake to remove the material, but the springy tines of the rake get caught repeatedly on the gnarly trunks of the hedge. This is no fun.

Then the cool logic of the male mind kicks into gear. Why not just set fire to the debris? The brisk spring breeze would quickly sweep the flames from one end of the hedge to the other, and surely the tough, woody trunks would suffer no ill effects from the brief exposure to the heat. After all, in the Caribbean they burn the cane fields to remove the dead leaves and grass before the harvest, and the stalks that hold the sweet sugar sap come through unscathed. Same principle, right?

So he whips out some matches and sets fire to the debris at the north end of the hedge, and in only a minute or two the wind has fanned the orange flames through to the other end, leaving only a slight residue of ash which will soon be washed away by spring showers. Mission accomplished.

About six weeks later, our hypothetical husband notices that, while every other plant in the back yard has either bloomed or leafed out, the hedge is still brown, dry, and dormant. In fact, closer examination reveals that it is as dead as a doornail.

He stares at the brittle branches for a few seconds, says "Huh!" and then goes to the lumber yard and buys two sections of decorative fencing which he installs in place of the lifeless hedge. Problem solved. Case closed. He never gives it another thought.

Fourteen years later, on an early spring day, our hypothetical husband prepares to go outside and do some yard work. As he heads for the door the wife calls to him: "You don't have any matches, do you?"

"No," he answers, patting his pockets. "Why?"

She trills cheerily: "Remember what happened to the hedge!"

SUNRISE ON THE RIDGE

I Am, Therefore I Plant

Every spring I wonder what motivates us to get out and start digging in the dirt, planting things. Is it some primitive instinct that harks back to the days before there were supermarkets filled with produce and convenience stores on every corner to fulfill our need for food?

That may be part of it, but I suppose there are other factors that come into play, depending on the history and experiences of each individual. Nevertheless, gardening is booming — even among city folks. From vegetables to flowers to herbs to "water gardening" (building a lily pond in your yard), providing plants, tools, seeds, fertilizers, and other necessities to those smitten by this hobby has become a multi-billion-dollar business.

Some would say it's because store-bought produce can't compare in flavor or texture to home-grown, naturally ripened fruits or vegetables. They certainly have a point. You could travel the world over, visit the most renowned gourmet restaurants on the planet, and never find a delicacy to surpass the luscious perfection of a fat, red, juicy, vine-ripened tomato, carried directly from the garden, still warm from the sun, sliced and sprinkled with a few grains of salt and pepper. Ummmmm!

Gardening helped a lot of rural residents survive the Great Depression in considerably more comfort than their big city cousins, and for many of us gardening is just a matter of routine. Our parents and grandparents had gardens, so we have gardens.

My father always demonstrated painstaking precision and enormous patience in laying out our garden. He liked to plant a large garden — a huge garden it seemed at the time. Using stakes and a ball of twine, he would create rows that were absolutely straight and evenly spaced while I fidgeted in the background, wishing we could just shove the seeds into the dirt and move on to something more entertaining.

Once the garden was planted, however, Dad seemed to lose interest. Layout and design were his specialties; hoeing and weeding were delegated to us kids. My sister and I used to sing while we hoed. We worked up some pretty good duets out there in the hot July sun. "We will have these moments to remember . . . ." one of those songs declared, but at the time neither of us thought we'd ever care to remember those moments spent chopping at the stubborn weeds firmly rooted in the hard yellow clay.

The worst experience came one summer when, in a serious lapse of judgment, I selected gardening as one of my 4-H projects. One day in late July, with the county fair rapidly approaching, Charlie Yeager, the county agricultural agent, dropped by the house for a surprise visit. He wanted to see how my garden was doing.

It was one of the most embarrassing moments of my young life, for my garden was not doing well at all. Oh, there were tomatoes and potatoes growing in there, but they were hard to spot amid the huge growth of weeds that had overwhelmed the entire plot and now swayed gently — three or four feet tall — in the hot summer breeze.

Charlie managed to pass it off without being critical. He always tried to find something positive to say, but this situation must have challenged him.

But time heals all wounds, and now I find myself spending cold January days thumbing through seed catalogs, fantasizing over color illustrations of "new and improved" vegetable varieties.

I don't have a large garden now — just a few tomato plants and green peppers. It's all time will allow. But someday I'll have a big garden with sweet corn and cabbage and carrots and peas and onions. I'll cut some stakes and buy a ball of twine, and with painstaking precision and enormous patience, begin marking off the rows . . . .

BUTTERFLY GARDEN

GET OFF MY BUMPER, YOU #!*&%S#!!!

Getting older and getting grouchier seem to go together. Or maybe it's just me. At any rate, I find I have less patience with certain aspects of life than I used to have — and I never did have very much, Judy tells me.

For example, the older I get the more idiot drivers there seem to be on our public streets and roads. Is it them or me? I'm pretty sure it's them.

Surely I'm not the only one who's noticed that drivers don't stop for a red light anymore — unless they're fourth or fifth in line when the light changes. In driver education class, we learned from Mr. Duffy that smart drivers stop when they see the light turn from green to yellow as they approach the intersection. No one driving today has ever heard such a suggestion. Watch next time. When the light turns red you'll see one, two, maybe even three more vehicles zoom on through! They seem very confident the cross traffic will wait for them. Idiots are always confident because they're too stupid to know they're idiots. But they can still get a driver's license.

Or how about turn signals? How much energy — or intelligence — does it take to move a turn signal lever half an inch? But there you sit, ready to pull out onto the highway, waiting . . . waiting . . . for an approaching vehicle that gets to within 10 feet of you — and turns off! No signal, of course. Idiots!

Don't even get me started on headlights. Part of that problem comes from new technology — new types of headlights that cast incredibly penetrating beams of light and are set at exactly the correct height to reflect off your rear view mirror when an idiot in a pickup truck or van climbs on your bumper, upset because you're only moderately exceeding the speed limit and he wants to go faster. Of course, the fact that you are now blinded tends to make you slow down, further increasing the moron's impatience.

And where can these people be going that is so all-fired urgent they have to drive 90 miles an hour to get there? No where. You can bet on it. They've probably just left work and are either headed home or headed to the local tavern, and gaining 30 seconds along the way isn't going to make any difference. In fact, you'll notice that nine times out of ten, in spite of their speed, you catch up to them at the next stoplight. Morons!

Maybe it's time we stopped talking and did something about it. Maybe we could get the legislature to consider setting up a new agency — a one-man bureau who would decide with absolute finality who gets to drive and who doesn't. The director of this agency would have to be the grouchiest, meanest, most opinionated old coot in Indiana.

And I know just the man for the job.

THE GREAT FISH SANDWICH CAPER

For many decades, until it finally was discontinued in the late 1970's, a carnival came to our little town every July. Actually, it was called the Soldiers and Sailors Annual Homecoming and Reunion, but most of us just referred to it as "the carnival."

For one week in July, carnival rides and "amusements" would be set up around the courthouse square, and crowds would flock to town to ride the rides, eat candy apples and cotton candy, try to win a teddy bear by throwing a baseball or shooting a basketball, or just visit with folks they hadn't seen for a while.

The Ferris wheel was always located on the corner of Walnut and Main Streets, and the merry-go-round was always at the corner of Cross and Main. The fish stand was located along the corner of the courthouse fence on Walnut Street across from the Ferris wheel. And it was the fish stand that caused all the commotion in our family one summer evening in the late 1940's.

One evening when I was four years old there had been some discussion about going downtown to the carnival and having fish sandwiches for supper, but for some reason the plan fell through, and we ended up having our usual homecooked meal around the dining room table.

But little Joey's appetite wasn't satisfied — all that talk had primed his taste buds for fish.

After dinner, I went outside to play. I was wearing a little yellow corduroy jumper-type outfit — short pants with a bib overall-type front; no shirt, and no shoes. For a while I sat and played in the bare spot under the elm tree in the back yard where I operated my toy cars and other vehicles in the sand. But a plan was hatching in my devious little mind.

After a while, I simply got up and headed down the path across what at that time was just a field of weeds between the back of our house and Bloomington Road. I wasn't sure exactly how I was going to do it, but I was going to get a fish sandwich. At one point I stopped and picked several large leaves off a horseweed, thinking I might offer them as currency, but then I threw them away, realizing that grownups probably wouldn't go for that.

I reached Bloomington Road and headed downtown, my little bare feet plopping along in the soft sand that collected along the edge of the blacktop. In no time at all I had made my way to Walnut Street and down the hill to Main Street.

There was no traffic light there in those days, but the town marshal (I think it was Clyde Boofer) was directing traffic, and I fell in with the crowd and made it across the street — right to the fish stand.

It was a wonderful establishment — full of delicious smells, sights, and sounds. Mounds of freshly fried fish were piled in glass windows above the counter, and the busy waiters would call out their orders — "Swim two!" they would cry — and the cook would slide two more filets into the cauldron of sizzling grease.

I stood there for a while before the proprietor noticed me. He was a ferret-faced man who was at the fish stand every year — he may have owned it, for all I know, because he was always there.

He looked down at me and asked, "What'll you have?"

"Fish sandwich," I replied.

"You want a big one or a little one?" he asked.

I didn't hesitate. "A big one."

He placed the pieces of fish in a bun, wrapped the sandwich in waxed paper, and handed it to me. And, without so much as a thank you, I took it and headed home.

(We wondered later what he must have thought and concluded that he probably assumed the little urchin with the dirty face and dirty feet belonged to some of the carnival people).

I ate my fish sandwich as I made my way up Walnut Street, but as I reached the top of the hill, here came my brother and sister, Bob and Carol Sue, looking for me, and I could tell right away that my adventure had not been favorably received at home. In fact, I learned that my mother had taken to her bed, distraught — certain that gangsters had kidnapped her baby boy. Dejected now, I threw the remainder of my fish sandwich into the roadside weeds and, closely guarded by my two older siblings, headed home to face the music.

Like many events which weren't considered funny at the time, the incident eventually became a part of our family lore and my primary claim to fame when stories were told. Inevitably, when July rolled around and the carnival came to town, someone would say, "Remember the time Joe got his fish sandwich?"

ARBOR WITH GOURD

PAINFUL TRUTHS FROM THE MOUTHS OF BABES

We seem to fall back on a standard collection of old clichés when discussing certain aspects of life. Without having to think, we roll out these comfortable old comments to fill up some of the holes and spaces in our daily dialogue. The weather is a good example. There's no originality involved, but when you want to make conversation what's easier than "Hot enough for you?" or "Looks like rain . . ." thereby putting the conversational ball in the other person's court.

And who hasn't heard someone say, "If you don't like the weather in Indiana, wait five minutes and it will change?" Some statements like that have been around so long and have been repeated so often that we make them a part of our personal repertoire even though, if we ever really thought about it, they may express something we don't even believe. Is the weather any more changeable in Indiana than it is in Illinois or Ohio or Michigan or Kansas? I don't know. But I wouldn't be surprised to learn that residents of those states make the same joke about where they live.

Like most things that have become part of our "conventional wisdom," these sayings are composed of a grain of truth topped with a liberal dollop of exaggeration. They usually contain a bit of humor, and that's probably why we adopt them — everyone likes to do the Will Rogers bit now and then.

There are several of these chestnuts that apply to the joys of being a grandparent — suggestions that being a grandparent is more fun than being a parent because you can spoil the grandkids and not have to live with the consequences or that the best thing about grandkids is that, after you enjoy them all day, they go home.

People repeat these, in various configurations, and we respond with a chuckle, a nod, or a grin, acknowledging the grain of truth and yet knowing that we don't really spoil them and we aren't really glad to see them leave.

The fact is that grandchildren provide a valuable service. All kids say the darndest things, but grandkids have a way of slicing right though all the layers of propriety to the very heart of the bitter truth.

Take little Sara, for example. She climbs up onto the Lazy Boy, gives you a surprisingly sharp slap on the stomach and scolds: "Bad belly! Bad belly!" That is followed by a few seconds of frowning, critical assessment and the pronouncement: "You're fat like Daddy."

We come out of the house getting ready to go to the store, and Megan looks up and asks: "Hey, Paw-paw . . . How come you drive a junky old car?"

No phony flattery here, folks. Grandkids tell it like it is. No holds barred. Let the chips fall where they may. If you can't take the heat get out of the kitchen. Take it or leave it.

True, you may be momentarily stunned when one of these gems of innocent revelation is first dropped on you, but, strangely enough, as time goes on you may find you have added them to your collection of most treasured moments. Grandparents are gluttons for punishment.

"Bad belly" has become a part of our family vocabulary — a signal that someone needs to get back on the "delicious shake for lunch" routine. And no one ever refers to the Chevy anymore except as "the junky old car."

And not all moments are the same. Lindsay bursts into the house during her first trip from the city to our country home, her eyes huge, holding her hands out as if measuring a large fish, and exclaims: "Grandpa! I was this close to a cow!"

Or there's little Alex, presenting a very persuasive argument that he not only knows how to drive the tractor but would be happy to change the oil for me.

Or Joshua, when his mom announces that it's time to leave, pleading: "I want to stay and help Grandpa."

We may be exhausted at the end of the day; our heads may be spinning slightly, but it's not true that we're glad to see them go.

Sorry, June —
October is the Perfect Month

The poet James Russell Lowell (1819-1891) asked the rhetorical question: "And what is so rare as a day in June?"

My answer would be: "Just about any day in October."

October is such a dramatic month, bringing with it all kinds of changes, an explosion of color, and a spiritual magnetism that makes us want to roam the fields and forests and get close to the earth.

Crisp breezes clear away the oppressive haze and humidity of summer; the more annoying varieties of insects give way to inoffensive grasshoppers and singing crickets, and the bright colors of pumpkins, apples, pears, persimmons, and yellow corn stir memories of earlier days and visits with grandparents when such bounty was picked fresh from the tree, vine, or stalk.

Other months may display their allure in more refined, subtle ways; in comparison October's cloak of many colors is almost too gaudy — the burnt gold of the hickory tree, the fiery orange of the sugar maple, and the multi-colored tapestry of black gum, sumac, and sassafras immodestly screaming, "Look at us! Take our picture! Aren't we beautiful?" October refuses to be taken for granted.

October skies also tend toward the spectacular, never understated. Is there any other time of year when the sky is that blue? Even on stormy days, some dazzling effects are created — a row of brightly colored trees glowing against a backdrop of massive blue-black storm clouds, made even more vivid by sunlight suddenly breaking through on the opposite side of the hill. As night approaches, the setting sun bathes those same clouds in slowly changing pastel shades of yellow, blue, lavender, and red, and as that scene fades to black a fat orange moon rises from behind the ridge and begins its trek across the night sky.

The winds of change are in the air. Wood ducks and geese suddenly appear on farm ponds and lakes, moving in silent swirls in the early morning mist rising from the water; deer make their way from the woods through the pasture to yet another woodlot, disturbed by hunters or by farm machinery moving through the ripe corn and soybean fields. Domestic animals' coats begin to thicken, reminding us that these golden days of autumn will be short-lived, soon to be replaced by the gloomy, wet chill of November.

To some people, autumn is a sad time — they see the falling leaves and withering grasses as symbols of death, and they long, instead, for spring and the resurrection. True, there are fleeting moments when a rush of fragrant windblown leaves triggers a brief flash of unexpected melancholy — thoughts of a long-lost friend or relative or fading images of college pennants flying and marching bands drumming, flaming leaves against the sky when we were all so young.

But to me October is a celebration, the grand finale in which all the promise of the spring and summer is gleaned from the fields, forests, and orchards and piled high on wagons, in baskets, and on tables, stored away in bins, cellars, and cupboards to see us through the dormant chill of winter to the start of another cycle.

October is bigger than life, a month when all the senses — sight, sound, taste, touch, and smell — are stirred and enticed by nature at its finest.

"Then, if ever, come perfect days . . . ."

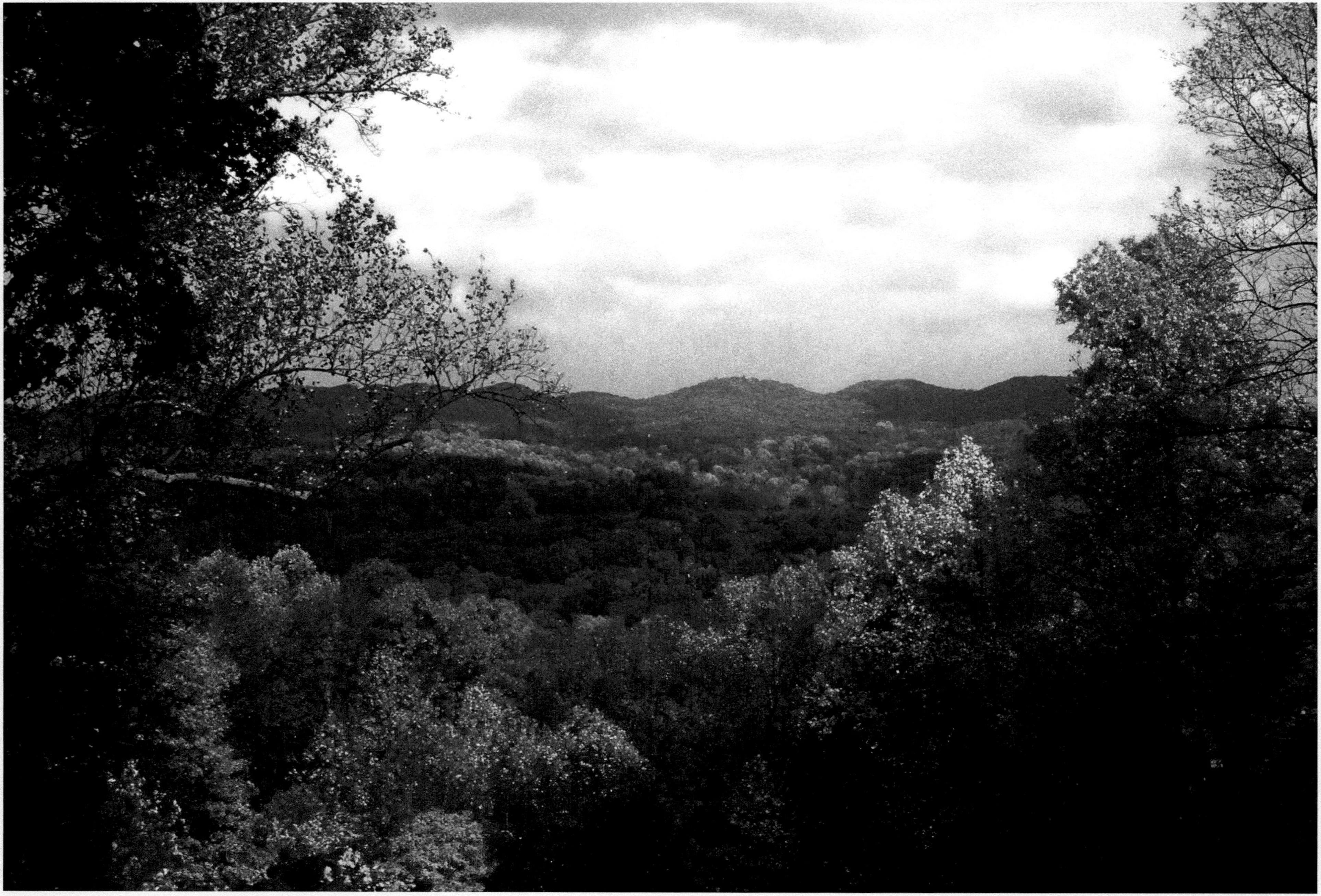

View from Skyline Drive

ANOTHER CRANK CALLER EXPOSED

Absentmindedness is an interesting thing. Everyone suffers from it on occasion while some of us display an absolute talent for it.

Its most frequent manifestation comes when Judy and I are in the car, supposedly headed out of town to some distant destination, and instead I turn and pull up in front of my office.

"Why are we stopping here?" Judy will ask, and I have to admit I have no answer. It's like the old work horse that, given free rein, automatically heads for the barn.

A more unusual example happened a couple of weeks ago. My son, Aaron, and I had gone to the city to pick up some stuff we had ordered for the house. When we got back to town I decided to stop at the office (on purpose this time) and call home to see if we needed to pick up anything at the grocery store. Aaron said he would wait in the car.

Inside the office, I went to the nearest desk phone, punched one of the three lines, and had just dialed the number when one of the other phones started ringing. I canceled my call home and punched the other line to take the business call.

"Good evening, The Banner," I answered. There was silence on the line.

"Hello, this is The Banner office . . . May I help you?" I tried again. No response.

"Stupid pranksters," I growled, slamming down the receiver. "Next they'll probably want to know if my refrigerator's running. [Then you'd better go catch it! Ha-ha-ha!]"

I tried my call again but, sure enough, while I was waiting for the connection The Banner phone started ringing again.

I was a lot less cordial this time as I punched line two. "The Banner!" I barked. Again, only silence. "This is getting really annoying," I thought. "Next they'll want to know if I have Prince Albert in a can. [Then you'd better let him out! Ha-ha-ha!]"

It was not until the third time this happened that it finally dawned on me that, instead of dialing my home number I had been dialing The Banner number. The jerk making the crank calls was me.

When I finally punched in the correct number, it was quite a relief to hear Judy's voice on the other end of the line.

It all reminds me of the story about the lady who was standing in the kitchen with a puzzled look on her face, and a family member asked what she was thinking about.

"The hereafter," the lady said.

"You're thinking about heaven?"

"No," she said. "I came in here for something, but now I can't remember what I'm here after!"

I know the feeling.

RECAPTURING THE MAGIC OF CHRISTMAS

Forgive me if I seem too often to speak of the way memories can be evoked by such things as a fleeting sound, a smell, or the feel of a cool breeze on the face, but it's a phenomenon I find fascinating. The most recent occurrence was a week or two ago during a period of snowy, cold weather. We were driving into town one night, and as I looked out over the blue-white fields of moonlit snow-covered corn stubble it was just as if I were seeing them from the back seat of my dad's old blue Pontiac, riding into town with him and Mom and a brother and sister or two, watching the cold countryside roll by from the warm safety of that heavy old car.

We might have been heading to the annual Christmas program at the old Walnut Street school — the building they tore down a few years ago. At that time — the early 1950's — the Christmas program was definitely the highlight of the year. We kids hadn't been ruined yet by television — we could still be dazzled by cardboard stars covered with glitter or awed by plywood cut-outs of manger scenes and palm trees, and shepherds wearing bathrobes, and we could be inspired by the sound of a hundred children's voices singing "Silent Night."

Preparations for the Christmas program went on for weeks in advance, anticipation reaching almost unbearable levels by the night of the event. In each classroom, pupils and their teachers — Miss Gladys, Miss Martin, Mrs. Carr, Mrs. DeLong, and all the others — worked on special projects, decorations, and displays which would be unveiled on that one special night as parents, brothers and sisters, and other guests visited each of the rooms before the start of the program to admire all the beautiful creations.

I don't know if this was done regularly, but one year, I recall, the school buses ran their routes that night. Dad was off on a job in Greenland or some place, so all of us — Mom included — boarded the school bus and rode into town to the Christmas program. It was kind of strange getting on the bus at night, and it was even more strange to see a few adults mingled with the kids who usually rode the bus, as well as some of their little brothers and sisters who weren't yet in school. And as the bus rolled along I'm sure we looked out onto those same cold winter cornfields and watched the stars glittering in the clear, crisp December night sky.

The format of the Christmas program never changed. A few lucky students (I secretly longed to be one of them) were chosen each year to enact scenes from the Christmas story on stage. During each scene, one of the classes (seated in the bleachers) would sing a couple of Christmas songs. The first grade might sing "Oh Little Town of Bethlehem" and "O Holy Night," and then there would be another scene on stage, and then the second grade would sing "It Came Upon a Midnight Clear" and "We Three Kings," and the tableaux and the songs would progress until the end of the story when the entire student body, faculty, and audience would join in an enthusiastic rendition of "Joy to the World" as the grand finale.

Oh, what a night it was. And when it was over, we headed home, still giddy from the spectacle of it all, our hearts and heads filled with music and images and feelings of peace on earth, good will to men . . . .

POVERTY RIDGE WINTER

SINGERS TRY TO 'OUT COUNTRY' EACH OTHER

We haven't watched much television since we moved out here to the ridge. That's because we don't have a real antenna yet, and we only get one channel that's clear enough to see. It's kind of nice, really, because we've been spending more time in the evening reading, listening to music, or just talking.

More than anything else we miss the morning news on the Indianapolis television station that we used to watch when we lived in town and had cable. It let us know — before we got to the newspaper office to start our day's work — whether anything major had happened during the night. Unfortunately, that's not the channel we get here in our new location, so we've started listening to the radio in the morning as a way of getting our news preview for the day.

Sometimes we listen to Robert Becker at WJAA because he's a friend of ours, and another old pal, Jim Plump, does a morning sports program there. Other times we listen to the other local station (we still call it WJCD even though we know it has new call letters) because Bud Shippee and Blair Trask are friends, too, and if there's a big news story Bud will usually have it. Blair just reads the birthdays and plays country records.

Having listened to these country top 40 selections for several weeks now, we've begun to have some troubling suspicions about the new breed of country singers. In fact, we're getting the impression that some of them are, as my dad would say, "as phony as a three-dollar bill."

They're all groomed and polished and packaged by multi-million-dollar companies with only one aim in sight: to make more millions. But, ironically, part of this high tech packaging appears to involve a competition to see which performer can come across as the most humble, down home, ordinary good ol' boy who ever shook the hayseed out of his hair. Some of them have taken on hillbilly accents so thick you can barely figure out what they're saying. Nobody really talks like that. They're making $80 million a year, but they want us to think they just fell off a pumpkin wagon in Mayberry.

It has led me to wonder if, hidden in the dark underground recesses beneath the MCA building in Nashville, there's a secret room where diction coaches help aspiring country singers learn to talk like morons.

Diction coach: Here, read this.

Aspiring singer: I love you.

Diction coach: No, no, no! It's: Ah luv yew!

Aspiring singer: I just can't get it right.

Diction coach: No, no, no! It's: Ah jist cain't git it rat!

Well, maybe I'm imagining things, but the next time you listen to a country music station, check it out. You'll hear a lot of young fellows working awfully hard to sound like real country bumpkins. Maybe if they didn't try so hard they'd be more convincing.

OLD STORE AT NORMAN

YOU NEVER KNOW WHO YOU'LL RUN INTO

Jack Kemp, a former congressman and candidate for Vice President, spoke last week at the local Republicans' Lincoln Day dinner. He's a very entertaining speaker — down to earth, fond of humor, and fascinated with history. And he has the ability to share his enthusiasm and philosophy of life with the audience.

Listening to Kemp's speech, I was reminded of the time I met another famous Republican — under less than auspicious circumstances.

In the summer of 1958 my dad got a job maintaining the trucks and other heavy equipment being used to build the Glen Canyon Dam in northern Arizona, and we all piled into the old blue Pontiac and headed west.

The construction site was out in the middle of a desert of red sand and rocks on the edge of a Navajo reservation. The town of Page was being constructed from scratch as the dam project went along, but at that point there wasn't much to it. The school, for example, was in a metal warehouse building. They had an outdoor theater, but it wasn't a drive-in; it was a walk-in theater. It had a wooden fence around it so you couldn't stand outside and watch without paying, and on the inside were wooden benches. So you sat there under the starry Arizona sky watching the movie, which was fine except for the night they showed the science fiction film about giant irradiated insects that were attacking people in a desert landscape just like the one we were sitting in. I walked home pretty fast that night.

The construction site was kind of neat, from a kid's point of view. The only way to get from one side of the river to the other was a footbridge made out of woven metal resembling a chain link fence. Steel cables supported the bridge floor, and the woven material came up on each side to form waist-high walls so you wouldn't fall off. This bridge hung several hundred feet above the river, and some folks found it disconcerting that you could see through the mesh floor straight down to the bottom of the canyon where the big payloader trucks looked like toys. But for a kid it was exciting. Of course, we weren't allowed to play on the bridge, but we could go a little farther down along the canyon and explore. It's a wonder I survived the summer without plummeting from the canyon edge to the river far below.

For a while that summer I ran around with a kid whose name I don't remember now. He was a kind of scruffy kid who, like everyone else, was there because his dad was in construction. But he had a bicycle.

One day we were riding around town on his bicycle with me pedaling and him sitting on the handlebars. He was wearing those flip-flop rubber sandals or thongs, as some people call them. We had just turned onto one of the new streets in the new town of Page when suddenly the bicycle did a complete end-over-end flip, and we landed on the pavement. It seems my new-found friend had gotten his toes stuck in the spokes of the bicycle's front wheel.

I wasn't hurt, although it took me a minute to recover from the shock of the sudden spill, but my friend was moaning and wailing with considerable volume, holding his toes and writhing around in the street.

About this time a virtual parade of big shiny black automobiles turned the corner and came upon the scene of our little accident. Several men in dark suits got out of the vehicles and walked around, asked a few questions, and apparently figured out what had happened.

My friend was still wailing.

After a few minutes another car pulled up, and an older gentleman got out and approached the men in suits. One of those men stepped forward, took the new arrival by the arm, and escorted him over to a tall, distinguished looking man who had just stepped out of one of the cars.

"Doctor," the escort said, "I'd like you to meet Senator Goldwater."

The doctor and the Senator shook hands and exchanged a few pleasantries, and then the doctor turned his attention to my friend, who was still making a lot of noise. His injuries were not serious, of course, although I'm sure his toes were pretty sore for a while.

Anyway, from that time on whenever the name of Barry Goldwater came up I could say that I had met him, although I usually avoided explaining just how our paths had crossed.

AUTUMN CREEK

Yes, Virginia — You Should Have Seen This

I know Christmas is past, and most of us have moved on to other things, but I wanted to comment on something that happened just before Christmas in our little town.

I was parked near the intersection of Main Street and Walnut Street, waiting for Judy to complete a transaction at the bank, when who should come strolling down the street but Santa Claus!

I know we've all seen Santa lots of times — in department stores, in parades, at parties — but it seemed different having him appear like this, unexpectedly, and not in connection with any special event.

There he was — red suit, boots, and all — just walking along the street in front of Nierman's law office, looking relaxed and laid-back, in no particular hurry (which was surprising considering how quickly the big day was approaching). When he got to the corner he had to stop for the light, and he stood there, waving to the occupants of passing vehicles, all of whom smiled and waved back excitedly.

It was a wonderful little scene that, although lasting only a few seconds, was filled with warmth and joy and the spirit of the season.

I didn't see many children in those passing vehicles. Most were adults, and every one was grinning from ear to ear and waving at Santa, as excited as four-year-olds — from a lady in a business suit to a grizzled, bearded deer hunter in a muddy four-wheel-drive truck. Some of them honked their horns.

Then the light changed, Santa ambled across the street, turned north (of course!) and disappeared from view, leaving at least eight or 10 folks in a happier mood than they had been a few seconds earlier.

I wish you all could have been there.

It's Not a Habit — It's a Hobby

Shortly before we moved out here to Poverty Ridge I developed an interest in cigar smoking. Let me hasten to add, however, that — like President Clinton — I never inhale. I just kind of puff on the cigar and enjoy watching the smoke billow and swirl around me, and I enjoy the aroma.

I know most people think cigars are smelly, nasty things. They can be, but they don't have to be. I enjoy the smell of cigars — mainly, I think, because my dad smoked cigars, and that warm, pungent aroma often triggers pleasant memories. You could always tell when he entered a room because that faint fragrance of traditional green Mennen aftershave mingled with cigar smoke preceded him. It was a comforting, reassuring smell that came to represent home and security.

Still, I try not to inflict my new hobby on others. Judy has a genuine fear of second-hand smoke and, of course, I respect that. And neither of us wants the house to smell like stale smoke. So most of my cigar sampling takes place in the great outdoors.

I'm sure there are many who would be happy to point out the stupidity of voluntarily indulging in a tobacco product in this age of enlightenment. I would tend to agree when it comes to cigarettes, having been a cigarette addict many years ago. Those things'll kill you. But that's cigarettes. They represent the opiate of the masses — machine made, mass-produced, and — until the government raised the tax umpteen times — cheap. Cigars are a horse of a different color.

Like many other products which come from nature — fine wine, coffee, tea, even maple syrup — good handmade cigars are the result of climate, soil, and the skill of the artisan who creates the final product. To appreciate a fine cigar, you must be open to recognizing the raw material, the expertise, and the effort that went into producing it.

So that's what I'm doing as I sit here on the back porch, cigar in hand, watching the last lingering glow of a January sunset reflecting off the icy surface of the little pond. A bitter winter wind howls around the corner of the house and snatches the fragrant smoke away into the approaching darkness. The temperature is falling fast.

I'll sure be glad when spring comes.

THE 'GLORY DAYS' WEREN'T ALWAYS SO GLORIOUS

Every April when the local chapter of the Red Cross sponsors an old timers' county basketball tournament, I find myself thinking about my high school years at "old BHS."

The sports scene was a lot different 40-some years ago at the pre-consolidation rural high school. We had boys basketball, baseball, track, and cross country. There was no organized football, volleyball, or tennis, and there were no girls' sports. The girls had GAA (Girls Athletic Association) that met once a week after school.

For the boys, competition for a spot on the various teams wasn't as intense as it seems to be today. Of course, there were a lot fewer kids. And most of us weren't that good, so we weren't worried about trying to get a basketball scholarship or even making a college team. Some of us didn't even know such things were available; we were just happy to be on the team and get a few minutes' playing time, especially if the girlfriend of the moment happened to be watching.

Still, we believed the things the coaches drummed into us about good sportsmanship, fairness, and unselfishness. We even believed them when they told us that if we worked hard enough we could beat anybody. The statistics might have contradicted that.

One year when we were in the seventh grade, a team from the largest school in the county beat us 43-3. Danny Nowling was our high point man with one basket. I forget who made the free throw.

In the opening game of my freshman season, I made 13 points — a career high as it turned out. A few days later at practice, I overheard another team member muttering to a friend that I was a "shotgun." Being the sensitive youth that I was, I was devastated. A shotgun! Me? I was mortified; tarred with the most nefarious label of high school sports. A shotgun!

Determined that no one ever have any possible reason to refer to me in such a way again, I gave up shooting and devoted myself to playing tenacious defense and rebounding. I'm sure Coach Sommers must have wondered what happened, and, looking back, of course, I wish I had told him. I'm sure he would have laid the "shotgun" concerns to rest very quickly.

But even though I didn't score much, I continued to make the team. I remember during a time-out the coach saying: "Rebounding's the only thing keeping you in there, Persinger!"

Born to rebound; that's me.

I wasn't so aggressive on offense, however. One day at practice we were running some half-court plays, and I posted up at the foul line and received a pass from one of the guards. But when I pivoted to face the basket, my defensive man snatched the ball out of my hands.

My cousin, Jim Blevins, was the varsity coach that year, and he immediately blew his whistle and came striding toward me with a very disgusted look on his face.

"What's the matter with you, Persinger?" he roared. "Don't let someone take the ball away from you like that!" He picked up a ball and demonstrated as he gave me some personal instruction. "When you catch that ball, get those elbows out and come around like you mean business. If you bust the other guy's nose, I'll lend him a towel."

Well, his words weren't lost on me. Hey, I was ready! I was tough! I was mean! Grrrr!

We started the play again. The guards passed the ball around, and I moved into position. Here came the pass. I grabbed the ball firmly in front of my chest. Ferocious now, I pivoted strongly toward the basket — and slammed my nose into Tom Bartels' elbow.

With blood streaming, I wandered toward the sidelines.

"Hey, coach — will you lend me a towel?"

SYCAMORE SKELETONS

Appeal of Hunting Seems to Have Dimmed

Since we moved from town out to Poverty Ridge, I've discovered I have mixed feelings about hunting.

As a young boy, I used to go hunting sometimes with my dad and my two older brothers. Back then people hunted rabbits and squirrels and quail — deer hunting had not yet become the fad it is today. I never turned down a chance to go since it was pretty special just to be invited to tag along. But, because I didn't have the benefit of any kind of proper gear, those excursions often ended with me trudging through snow-covered cornfields with cold, wet feet and numb fingers, praying that we would soon head for the warm car and home.

Still, I continued to pursue the sport for several years after graduating from high school and leaving home. I grew to prefer squirrel hunting, probably because it takes place in the nicest time of year — early fall — when it's pleasant just to be out in the woods and there's no danger of frozen feet. Another plus is that you can usually find plenty of squirrels, so you don't come home empty handed.

Anyway, when we moved out to the country, I thought I might get involved in hunting again. I even began looking at guns in some of the various catalogs we receive and checking out the newspaper ads from sporting goods stores. I gave a lot of thought to what kind of gun I should buy. If I bought a rifle for squirrels, then I would have to buy a shotgun for rabbits, quail, and grouse — and deer, if I decided to get involved in that. Or I could just buy a shotgun and use it for all those things, but then the question becomes what gauge: 12 or 20? Or I could buy a muzzleloading rifle and limit my hunting to deer and squirrels . . . Or how about trying a bow and arrow?

So I pondered and debated, and in the meantime we moved into our little house and began enjoying the sights and sounds of the country.

One day in October I discovered we had some visitors on the little pond. In the gray, flat early morning light it took me a while to make them out, even with binoculars. They were wood ducks — five of them — two males and three females, and they were there every morning for about three weeks. I wanted to get a good picture of them, but they were too skittish for me to get close enough, even with a telephoto lens.

One Sunday morning I was sitting on the back step after breakfast when, just beyond what would be considered our "lawn," two fox squirrels came tearing down the side of a big oak tree, chasing each other over the ground and up and around just having a big time and paying no attention to me at all. It gave me a nice feeling watching them.

Several weeks later, Judy and I went for a Saturday afternoon walk and, at the lower edge of our property next to the cornfield, two deer suddenly bolted out of a thicket and went bounding off across our property and the neighbor's place, finally disappearing into the woods, white flags flying. We stood and watched, delighted. Then, a couple of weeks after that, I got home one evening before dark and decided to see if there might be a deer in that same spot. As I approached, six deer exploded out of the brush and headed off across the cornfield in a kind of bobbing and weaving dance that made it hard to count them. It was exciting, and it made me wish I could get them to do that sometime when all the grandkids were here to see it.

So I'm having mixed feelings about hunting. Come next fall, I may decide to give it a try. Or I may decide it's more fun just observing those creatures in their natural setting or trying to "capture" them with my camera. It's one of those things I'm going to have to think about for a while.

BETTER DAYS GONE BY

WHEN BAD THINGS HAPPEN TO SILLY PEOPLE

We're fortunate enough to have a nice pond on our property, and during the summer I try to keep the top of the dam mowed for the enjoyment of family members and neighbors who like to go fishing once in a while. At one end of the dam is a slender metal fence post that marks the property line. I usually try to mow around it as close as I can so I don't have to get off my garden tractor and do any actual manual labor.

On one particular Saturday, I made a cut along one side of the post and backed up to make another swipe, but when I stepped on the tractor's clutch/brake pedal, nothing happened! That is, the tractor didn't stop — didn't even slow down! — and I suddenly found myself going over the edge of the dam backwards.

Now, if you've seen many dams, you know that the grassy side away from the water is usually pretty steep, and this dam is no exception — in fact, on a normal day I would not have the nerve to drive down it in a forward gear because of the likelihood that the garden tractor would gain too much speed and overturn.

So here I am, yelling "Yipee Ki-Yi" and three or four other things I can't mention here, riding this wild red Wheel Horse backwards down the horrendous slope. I only regret that I didn't have a cowboy hat to wave in the air, rodeo-style.

Actually, in the first split second that I felt the tractor going over the edge I thought of how this was going to look on the front page of The Banner: "Stupid Newspaperman Makes Mincemeat of Himself While Riding Mower Backwards Down Steep Dam Incline." What an embarrassing way to go!

Fortunately, I had enough presence of mind to turn off the ignition (which slowed the tractor enough that I was able to keep it from overturning) and to throw the lever to stop the whirling mower blades. From that point, I managed to inch my way to the bottom of the dam (still backwards) where I sat, breathing rapidly, for a while until I could pry my fingers off the steering wheel.

No harm done, but it was enough of a close call to make me stop and ponder how quickly a situation can go from boring routine to heart-pounding danger, especially when some of our labor-saving machines are involved.

The other accident happened on Labor Day and indirectly involved our kayak. Yes, we now have a kayak, but don't ask why — that's a subject for another column.

We decided that Labor Day would be the perfect time to take our new kayak on a cruise down White River which passes just a couple of miles from Poverty Ridge. It was a definite learning experience. For example, we learned that, for our first trip, we should have been less ambitious in choosing the distance we would go. Our inexperienced muscles began to scream less than halfway through the seven-mile journey. We also learned that, on a day when the temperature will be in the mid-90's, you should start out early in the morning or late in the afternoon so you could have at least some chance of being in the shade part of the time. We started at mid-day and baked in the hot sun for the entire distance.

Even at that, it was a pleasant enough trip. We returned home tired and hot, but feeling pretty good about our excursion. But then, as we were putting the kayak away in the barn, I stepped on an old piece of lumber with a big nail in it, and the nail went right through the sole of my tennis shoe and into the ball of my foot. In less than a second the day had gone from carefree pleasure to depressing incapacitation.

We decided I could wait until our family physician's office opened the next day to get a tetanus shot, so I made it to the doctor's office about 11 a.m. A nurse left me in the examining room, and when I took off my shoe I was shocked to see how swollen my foot had become. It was now a big fat foot with big fat toes, the skin stretched tight to cover it.

Dr. Calhoun came in and started to make a joke, but then he saw my foot and became more serious. He said the swelling indicated it was already infected, and he would prescribe some high-powered antibiotics to stop the infection. Otherwise, he commented, "You could end up in the hospital and have to have surgery."

Being the writer/dreamer/actor/ham that I am, I immediately began to picture myself in a hospital bed, awakening from the anesthetic, clutching at the empty space beneath the sheets and screaming, "Where's the rest of me?" in my best Ronald Reagan "King's Row" performance.

But, of course, the medicine worked, the swelling went away, and all I had to suffer was a week or so of limping around and having to think twice about whether making the trip from the family room to the kitchen for a cup of tea was worth the effort. But, again, it was a learning experience as I realized that, if such a minor thing could interfere so much with routine activities that I always took for granted, how devastating a really serious disability would be. I don't think I would cope with that very well. And I have a greater admiration now for those who do.

KEEP THOSE CARDS AND LETTERS (AND CATALOGS) COMING IN

I have to confess: I'm a junk mail junkie. While most people mutter and fume about all the unsolicited materials they receive, I hurry to the mailbox each morning with eager anticipation, hoping to find it bursting at the seams with all manner of brightly printed catalogs, brochures, and bulky envelopes that scream "You may already be a winner!"

Mainly I enjoy catalogs — which is odd because I'm not a shopper. After 10 minutes at the mall I'm exhausted and ready to go home. I enjoy catalogs the same way I enjoy magazines: I like to look at the pretty pictures — rich full color photographs of everything from flower gardens to hunting and fishing equipment to luscious-looking platters of food.

I enjoy pictures that show how a tiny rototiller (that I can lift with one hand!) will allow me to cultivate between narrow rows of vegetables or how reproductions of paintings by the old masters (on real canvas!) look almost as good as the originals or how a special deck awning can easily be unfurled when the sun is shining and then rolled up when the sun goes down.

I look at some catalogs the same way television viewers enjoy "Lifestyles of the Rich and Famous." For some reason, I enjoy looking at pictures of $800 fly rods even though I would never buy one even if I had that kind of money. It's fun to marvel over a box of cigars that sells for $380 or a piece of garden statuary listed at $2,500. (Someday I hope to produce a television show called "Lifestyles of the Poor and Obscure," but that's another story.)

I suppose the time spent leafing through catalogs is a form of window shopping. We stop, look, admire, joke about the exorbitant price, chuckle, and move on to the next page just as if we were moving on down the sidewalk in front of a traditional store.

And that's the other side of the coin. From the catalog company's point of view, I'm a big waste of their paper, ink, and postage because I rarely ever buy anything. ("Just looking, thank you.") Like most empty nesters, if there's something I really, really want I've probably already got it, and if I don't have it I probably don't need it. I'm a catalog copy writer's worst nightmare — the non-consumer.

Some of these companies are getting wise to me, too. Lately I've been getting catalogs with a bright sticker attached warning that, if I don't order something this time, they will take me off their mailing list. The good part is that in the same day's mail I got a catalog showing nothing but other catalogs I could order, and I spent at least an hour going through and checking the new catalogs I would like to receive — western wear, flower seeds, nothing but neckties, old movies on video, replicas of swords and pistols, cooking utensils, garden furniture, camera equipment, stuff from Australia, power tools, Pacific Northwest smoked salmon . . . .

I hope they all have lots of color pictures.

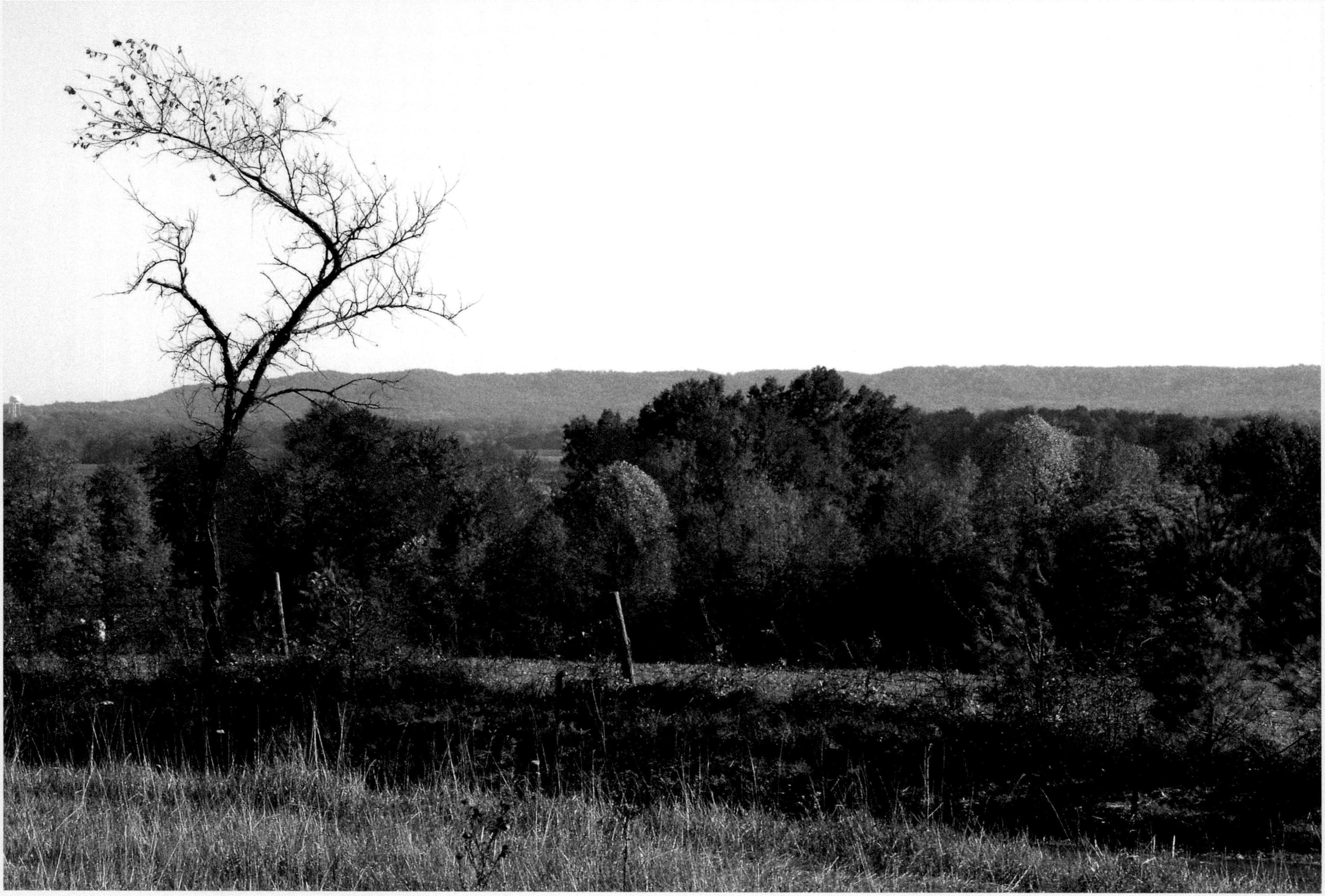

The View from Poverty Ridge

Most Lessons Learned after Graduation

Springtime is graduation time, and for many of us the sight of seniors in their caps and gowns triggers a flood of memories.

Like most traditions, commencement exercises have their roots in the past as much as in the present, and that twinge of sadness we feel may be as much for our own lost youth as for the seniors who are leaving their childhood days behind.

In many ways, the current class faces a darker, more threatening world than was anticipated by the class of 1962 — the class with which my own memories lie. But the current crop of seniors also may be equipped with more realistic expectations. We led a pretty sheltered life in our little town 40 years ago, and some of us were pretty naive. We were truly "rebels without a clue."

I remember one afternoon when Roger Hartman and I were sitting in the loft of the little barn that used to stand out behind the Lutheran Church. We were smoking pipes and watching a thunderstorm sweep across the fields. We were smoking pipes, I think, because we saw them as symbols of the intellectual class and, as college-bound scholars who had picked up our share of academic awards, we wanted very much to be viewed as part of that group.

As we puffed on our pipes and watched the clouds of Cherry Blend smoke waft out across the pasture toward the property where the new high school would one day stand, we talked about what we would study in college and what careers we would pursue. And I remember that we agreed if we could attain the luxurious salary of $15,000 a year we would be able to afford a fabulous bachelor pad in the city (and the latest hi-fi stereo and a sports car), and life would be perfect.

We didn't have a clue.

In fact, when the class held its first reunion in 1972, the first thing Tom Eastin said to me was: "We didn't know anything, did we, Persinger?" And he knew that I knew exactly what he meant.

We received a good education at "old BHS" — we were well versed in math, English, science, and history. But many of us were not at all prepared for the realities of full-time employment, marriage, debt, parenthood, the Vietnam war, illness, infidelity, divorce, drug and alcohol abuse, the death of parents, and all the other difficult lessons of adulthood.

We left high school filled with optimism and dreams, certain that the world would soon take note of us. And we returned for that reunion ten years later realizing that the world plays by its own rules and doesn't make exceptions for dreamers or fools.

But as time went on we learned. We adapted. We coped. We put some of those dreams on the shelf, buried some, and others we gave to our children. We went to work every day, paid our taxes, and went to the polls in November. We endured dance recitals, little league games, band concerts, and PTA meetings. We went to church, participated in community organizations, and gave to the United Fund.

And as we plodded on, the painful revelations of that first ten years receded into the distance and were gradually replaced by a more comforting discovery: that making the world a better place is more often accomplished in tiny increments than in dramatic leaps.

Fame and fortune had eluded us. We would never have our faces on the cover of Time; would never receive an Academy Award or a Nobel Prize. Our names would never become household words. But in small ways, day by day, year by year, like drops of water wearing away a stone, we had made a difference.

Perhaps this year's graduates can find some encouragement in the lesson we have learned: that decent, ordinary people leading decent, ordinary lives are our best hope for the future.

It's always been that way. We just didn't know.

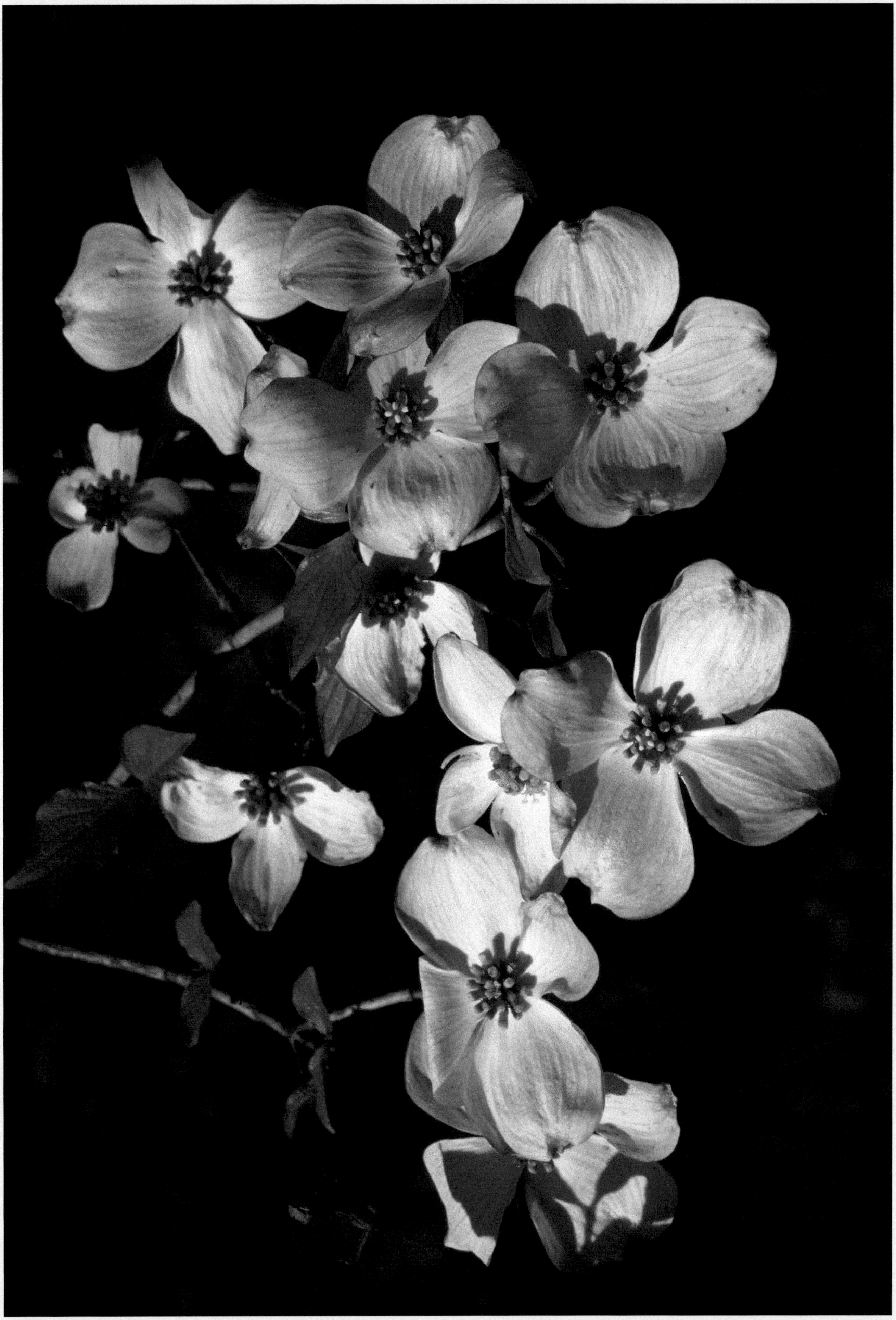

Pink Dogwood

Maybe I Should Have Stuck to Westerns

"I like you, Joe, but you're odd — you're just odd!"

It was over 40 years ago, and one of my high school girlfriends was breaking up with me — dumping me, kindly but firmly.

After she went inside and closed the door, I stood there on the front steps for a few seconds, collecting my thoughts. Odd? What a strange thing to say . . . .

Then I began to notice how the streetlights stretching away along Spring Street cast pools of light onto the pavement below, each circle of light smaller than the previous one as they receded into the distance. They reminded me of the scene that always closed "The Jimmy Durante Show" on TV. Remember? He would say goodnight to the audience and then, turning to the camera, tip his hat and utter that marvelously melancholy and mysterious farewell: "And goodnight, Mrs. Calabash — wher*ever* you are!" Then he would turn, and the lonely clown would slowly walk away, passing through successively smaller circles of light until, at last, he disappeared into the darkness.

I stepped down onto the sidewalk, rejected and alone, turned my collar to the wind, shoved my hands deep into the pockets of my windbreaker, and began my measured exit, passing from one small pool of light to the next. In my mind, I could hear the trembling tones of Mr. Acker Bilk's lonely clarinet playing "Stranger on the Shore" as I slowly disappeared into the night. Not a dry eye in the house . . . .

Odd? What could she have meant?

I don't know at what point my life was taken over by the silver screen, but it was very early. I remember at age four or five becoming furious when my new brother-in-law, Wendell, teased me by claiming that the wave in Roy Rogers' hair was created when he combed it over a bump on his head — a bump created when one of the bad guys smacked him. Those were fightin' words . . . .

A few years later Mom and my sisters and I went to the Royal Theater to see "From Here to Eternity." Actually, I probably shouldn't have been allowed to see it at that age, but I'm sure most of the adult themes went right over my head. I was greatly moved, however, by the plight of Montgomery Clift who, after being stabbed in the stomach during his fight with Sergeant Fatso, tries to get back to his barracks at Pearl Harbor, running and running, holding his hand on his wound, blood trickling through his fingers . . . .

By the time we got home that night I had such a pain in my side I could hardly walk — sympathy pains, I guess, because after a while they vanished without benefit of surgery.

Odd? I don't see why.

Theatrics seemed to spring naturally from the dream-like summers spent "up the hill" at my grandparents' house, less than 100 yards behind the home where I lived with my parents. With four sisters, two brothers, and assorted nieces, nephews, and cousins, there was rarely a shortage of playmates.

In those early days, we had no TV, and we entertained ourselves — sometimes magnificently. We wrote and staged plays for the adults, and when a cat or dog or bird died, we conducted impressive church services to lay them to rest. We played a card game called "Authors," and, as a result, although we may never have read "The Scarlet Letter," at least we knew who wrote it. My grandfather was a well read man who liked to quote poetry. ("Turn backward, turn backward, Oh time in thy flight, and make me a boy again, just for tonight" was one of his favorite lines.) We read Edgar Allen Poe and memorized his poems — for fun! ("Once upon a midnight dreary, while I pondered, weak and weary . . . .")

And we tried writing our own poems and stories. My first "novel" — a western, of course — included a descriptive passage about a troop of cavalrymen riding through a canyon, the desert dust turning to rivulets of mud as it struck the sweat on their faces. (I was going for gritty realism even at that early age.)

There was an old player piano (the "player" part long since broken) that we all pounded on periodically, and we sang . . . old time hymns, popular songs, tunes from other eras. I can remember sitting on the porch swing, drinking in the fragrance of morning glories and a riot of other old-fashioned flowers while my cousin, Alta Margaret, played "Beautiful Dreamer." Now there's a song you don't hear any more. Too bad.

Television did come, finally, in the mid-1950's. I remember the night they delivered the black-and-white set and placed it in the corner of the living room. The first thing we watched was the "Kraft Theater," a weekly program that brought live stage plays right into your living room! I remember seeing a very young Charles Bronson portraying a juvenile delinquent terrorizing a housewife. (At that time people used the term "juvenile delinquent" almost as if it was a very specific thing for someone to be, like a Boy Scout or a Methodist. Mainly, you knew someone was a juvenile delinquent if he wore a ducktail haircut and a black leather jacket and smoked cigarettes.)

Television was a miracle that brought us Sid Caesar, Bob Hope, Milton Berle, Jack Benny, and "Have Gun, Will Travel." When I was 13, Ed Sullivan introduced Brenda Lee to sing one of her hit songs on his show, and he mentioned that she, too, was just 13 years old. How I wished I could be there too, singing on "The Ed Sullivan Show."

But there was nothing like the movies. Whether it was at the Royal, the Majestic, or the Von Dee, settling back into your seat in the darkness and being enveloped by Technicolor images and amplified voices and music, learning about honor and bravery from John Wayne or seeing how Stewart Granger handled a fiery romance . . . .

Odd? Yes, I suppose that 17-year-old who lived in a celluloid world inside his own mind was a little odd. But he's seen some great shows.

PINES AND DOGWOODS

The Lights Are On But Nobody's Home

Well, we survived this winter's so-called blizzard (a mere squall compared to the real blizzard of 1978) with no permanent ill effects. The main thing we learned was not to buy more groceries than we could carry in one trip since we couldn't get the car more than a few feet into the driveway and had to walk the rest of the way down the lane to the house, eventually tramping a narrow path through the knee-high drifts.

Yes, the snow was pretty, and provided some nice photo opportunities, but — like everyone else — it didn't take us very long to get tired of it.

A natural event like that is probably a good thing every few years, though, because it puts us in our place. Human beings tend to be pretty arrogant most of the time, basking in the comfort of all our inventions and conveniences and luxuries, but it just takes one big roar from Mother Nature to bring it all to a halt and remind us we're not so powerful after all.

Some time ago, I wrote about absent-mindedness, using the example of the time at my office I kept dialing the wrong number and calling myself instead of calling home. Well, you'll be glad to know the beat goes on . . . .

A while back, I was helping with the local community theatre production of "Arsenic and Old Lace," and one night as I was leaving for a rehearsal, Judy said she would go into town too and catch up on some work at the newspaper office. So, after the 10-minute drive into town, I dropped her off at The Banner and went on to the Royal-off-the-Square theatre.

It wasn't a very good rehearsal. A couple of cast members obviously hadn't been spending any time memorizing their lines, much to the dismay of those who were trying to put their scripts aside and start working on their characterizations. And there were a couple of scenes where the movement of the actors on stage just wasn't working out right — everyone was ending up crowded together in one corner, practically standing on top of each other.

And it was getting late — 9:30 already, and we were trying not to rehearse later than 9 p.m. Things weren't going well at all.

As I left the theatre, all the problems with the production — and some possible solutions — were running through my mind. I could adjust the rehearsal schedule slightly so those folks who didn't know their lines could run through their scenes three or four times or as many times as it took for them to get it. That idea came to me as I drove through the west end of town, crossed the railroad tracks, and headed out into the country toward Poverty Ridge.

As for the difficulty with the staging, it occurred to me that in both troublesome scenes, the same character made his entrance through the cellar door, later to be joined by the other actors in the scene. All I had to do was get him to move to the left when he entered, hold his position, and make the other actors come to him. That would keep everyone in the center of the stage instead of bunched up in the corner!

By the time I turned off the state highway and was steering the Chevy through the curves to the top of the ridge, I was no longer so discouraged. It was about 9:45 when I turned into the drive, parked the car, and hurried into the house.

It was awfully quiet. No television going; no music on the stereo . . . I hung up my coat and tiptoed downstairs. Even more quiet . . . and dark! Had Judy gone to bed already? I leaned around the corner and peered into the bedroom. Nobody there.

"Where the heck is she?" I wondered, starting to feel somewhat alarmed.

Slowly, however, as I stood in the dim light of the hallway and looked into the unoccupied kitchen and dining room, alarm was replaced by a growing sense of impending stupidity.

I knew where she was. She was back at The Banner office wondering where I was! I grabbed the phone and called.

"Still there?" I asked. She said she was. "I'll be right there," I answered, and I grabbed my coat, ran to the car, and headed back into town, free — at least for the moment — of any thought that might distract me from my mission.

Except, of course, for trying to think of a less embarrassing explanation.

You Can Learn a Lot at the County Fair

Our county fair always brings with it some special memories. When I was a youngster, my family lived in a log house directly across the road from the entrance to the fairgrounds, so every August we all spent a lot of time at the fair.

In those days they had fireworks on the last night of the week-long exposition, and we could sit in our front yard and watch the ones that went high into the air — above the trees that stood between us and the grandstand. And we fell asleep each night to the sounds of the click-clacking rides on the midway, mingled in the distance with the barkers' voices, the squeals and laughter of the crowd, and music played over a loudspeaker.

One year a song they played frequently was "I'm Alone Because I Love You," a sentimental ballad that my mother said was an old song. But that week — at the peak of the 50's rock and roll era — that tune became one of my all-time favorites.

Food played an important part at the fair then as now, whether it was "western" sandwiches from one of the church-operated stands, cotton candy, or snow cones. It became a family tradition that each year during fair week we had to have some caramel corn and a pineapple whip ice cream cone.

A kid with a dollar could have a pretty good time back then — carnival rides were just a quarter. And a lot of time was spent just walking around looking at all the exhibits, the livestock, and — even in those pre-teen years — hoping to bump into that special girl you "liked" and hadn't seen since school let out in May.

And 4-H was an important component — rushing to the 4-H building on opening day to see what kind of ribbons you had won, and hurrying to the fair office at the end of the week to collect two or three dollars in premiums. (And then hurrying to the Western Auto store to spend it!)

One year the fair sponsored a "calf scramble." They released a bunch of young steers inside a temporary fence in front of the grandstand, and if you could rope one and pull it into a circle in the center of the arena, you could take the animal home, care for it for a year, and show it at the fair the next summer. Much to my parents' dismay, I caught an unruly Angus. Our family pastime for the next 12 months was chasing the steer each time it broke out of its pen. None of us was sorry to see it go when the next fair came around.

One year I was walking around the midway when the operator of one of the carnival games called me over.

"Pssst! Hey, kid. C'mere a minute!'

He made me an offer I couldn't refuse. He said he would provide me with quarters to play his game and, at the appropriate moment he would announce — so that everyone on the midway could hear — that I had won! Placing a huge teddy bear in my arms, he caused a great commotion, crying out, "We've got a winner! Here goes another one! A winner every time, folks! You're just in time — step right up and play!"

I would wander off through the gathering crowd, smiling and holding up my big prize for all to see, make a couple of slow laps around the midway, and then quietly return the teddy bear to the rear of the booth. This charade was repeated several times during the evening.

I don't remember how much I was paid for this service, but I was paid, and I figured I was doing pretty well to be making money at the fair instead of spending it.

But when I hurried home and broke this exciting news to my mother, she did not share my enthusiasm. She seemed concerned that working as a shill at the carnival would be the first fatal step leading me into a life of crime that would end with me in the big house doing life without parole. What I saw as a lark she saw as fraud, and that was the end of my carnival career.

So, a couple of years later, when I worked as a parking attendant at the fair, and Friday Robison took us all to the girlie show, I kept it to myself.

Words, Meanings, and Lawn Mower Men

Words are amazing. They can convey such an incredible range of thoughts, emotions, and subtle nuances of meaning. They can win battles, change history — and sometimes get you in a lot of trouble.

If you say someone is frugal, it's a compliment; if you say they're a pennypincher, it's not.

If you say someone is ambitious, it's usually taken in a positive way; if you say they're "pushy" it's a criticism.

If you say someone chuckled, it has a friendly sound; if you say they chortled, it makes them sound a little goofy.

There are some phrases that have found their way into the language in recent years that, hopefully, will find their way out again in the near future — terms such as "significant other," "chair" (instead of chairman), and "level playing field" (to mean fairness).

And while we're at it, why do television newscasters always say: "We're back in a minute with more news?" They all do it, but why? Is there some problem with saying "We'll *be* back . . . . "

And why do they say a person was injured *after* his car struck a bridge? Wasn't he injured *when* his car struck the bridge? Or did something else happen to him after the crash and, if so, what?

And why do so many sports writers talk about teams getting "untracked" when they're trying to suggest the team is doing well? Untracked means derailed, which is not a good thing. Don't they mean "on track?" When you get back on track, you're doing better.

Some combinations of words can fill our hearts with dread — phrases such as "I don't want to criticize, but . . ." or "I know you're busy, but . . . . "

Other phrases can bring us at least a fleeting moment of happiness — things like "your table is ready now" or "it's not broken, just sprained."

But, to me, at least, there is one phrase that has become so dreaded, so despicable and depressing, that I hope never to hear it again. (Although the odds of escaping it indefinitely are pretty slim).

The horrible phrase that carries the power to cast anyone into the depths of despair?

It'll cost more to fix than it's worth.

I have heard that pronouncement too many times, always from a repair person who seems barely able to contain his glee — the auto mechanic, the appliance repairman, the lawn mower man.

It'll cost more to fix than it's worth.

I haven't heard it yet from my doctor, but it's just a matter of time.

Speaking of lawn mower men, I stopped by my local power equipment dealer recently to have my blades sharpened, and while I was waiting I decided to strike up a conversation with the proprietor, Jim Cooper. So I said, "You know, I'm either going to have to cut back on the area I'm mowing or I'm going to have to get a bigger tractor."

Now, most garden tractor salesmen, given that kind of opening, would immediately usher you over to the 20-horsepower deluxe model with roll bars, headlights, cruise control, and hydraulic everything, and start calling your bank to arrange financing. But being a slow-talking, easy-going cowboy kind of guy (complete with droopy handlebar mustache), Jim pondered my remark for what seemed like several minutes and finally drawled: "Well, my advice to you would be to cut back on your mowing."

Then his sidekick, Sarge Richey, pointed out that it would cost a lot less to fence in my place than it would cost for a new garden tractor/mower. Then, he said, I could get some sheep to mow the grass and some goats to trim the hedges, and I would have a lot more time to go fishing.

Talk about your hard sell!

Then this veered off into a discussion about how hard it is to get things repaired nowadays, and they pointed out how annoying it is to them when people bring in generic implements needing work when there are signs all over the shop saying "We service the brands we sell."

With the proliferation of discount stores selling a variety of no-name garden tractors, lawn mowers, and chain saws, Jim noted, "We're refusing to work on more and more stuff all the time."

So, even though you may not be able to talk them into selling you a mower or working on your off-brand chainsaw, you might want to stop in at Cooper's occasionally . . . just for the entertainment.

OCTOBER FARM FIELD

MEN HEAR JUST FINE (IF THEY'RE LISTENING)

To all the men out there: I'll bet you can recall a time (or, more likely, many times) when you've been reading the newspaper or watching a television show when — all of a sudden, completely out of the blue — your wife asks, "You haven't heard a word I've said, have you?"

Now, you could just be honest and say, "Why, no, Dear. I wasn't even aware you were talking to me," but I wouldn't advise it.

It's best just to say, "Sure I was, Dear, but I missed that last part. What was that?"

If she's like most women she'll repeat the whole thing, and then you'll be up to speed on the current topic.

As we've noted before, and as observers have noted for thousands of years, men and women are different. Women, for example, can eat, play bridge, watch television, serve dessert, crochet a sweater, listen to the radio, remove bubblegum from a kid's hair, and carry on a conversation with four other women — all at the same time. Men like to focus on one thing until it's done and then move on to the next.

More times than I care to remember my wife and I have been in the car en route to some event when she would engage me in conversation. Then, moments later, she would interrupt the discourse to point out that I had driven right past the place we were going. She simply doesn't understand that I have to focus on one thing at a time. I can drive or I can talk — I can't do both at the same time.

She even makes fun of the way I eat, consuming all the potatoes first, then the meat, then the green beans — again, focusing on one thing at a time. Normal people, she points out (meaning women), like to take a bite of this and then a bite of that and keep mixing it up. Yuck!

But going back to the conversation aspect, the accumulation of these various episodes has led to her dropping subtle hints that I may need to have my hearing checked. A typical female reaction. There is nothing wrong with my hearing.

By the way — not to change the subject again, but have you noticed all those television commercials with Bob Dole talking about "reptile dysfunction?" What is that about, anyway? I can't imagine there are enough people who keep turtles and snakes and lizards and such as pets that it would pay to run those expensive TV commercials. I tell you, this whole world is getting weird.

But back to the hearing thing. All this reminded me of an old joke. Two friends meet on the street and one of them begins babbling about his new hearing aid and how wonderful it is.

"It's the greatest thing I've ever found," he boasts. "It's changed my whole life. Why, I can hear things now I didn't even know I was missing."

"Well, that's great," his friend responds. "What kind is it?"

The first fellow looks at his watch and replies, "Oh, about four-thirty."

DOWN BY THE POND

Once a Hillbilly Always a Hillbilly

In the early 1950's kids in our school district went from first grade through sixth grade in an 1890's-era building on Walnut Street — the building with a distinctive half-circle window, the building that was torn down a number of years ago during the most recent middle school renovation, the building where my parents met and fell in love a generation earlier.

During the winter of 1951-52, my second grade class was located in a room on the south side of that building, on the main floor. We sat in those traditional elementary school desk/chair combinations, furniture that obviously had served many classes before us, some of the desktops carved with initials or simply scarred from years of use. The desks still had a place for an ink well, although that degree of classic penmanship was no longer required, so there was no ink.

The room had wood floors made of narrow boards, maybe two inches wide, and every afternoon when school let out you would see the janitor scattering a kind of oily sawdust cleaning material over the floors and then sweeping it up. If you were bored, sitting in your little desk/chair on a sleepy afternoon, you could let your arm dangle low, and drag the sharp tip of your pencil along the crack between those boards and dredge up a black line of ages old dirt and sawdust stuff. I can still smell the cedary aroma of it.

Along the east side of the classroom there was a cloakroom — a term you don't hear much any more. It was just a long, narrow hallway, really, that children could pass through when they arrived in the morning or came in from recess, providing a place to hang your coat and a shelf for the lunch you brought from home.

It also was a room filled with winter smells — the co-mingled fragrance of ice and snow melting off rubber galoshes and seeping into that oily wood floor, the smell of wet wool, and the aromas of peanut butter and jelly or baloney sandwiches, apples, and oranges in brown paper bags or tin Roy Rogers lunchbuckets.

Our teacher that year was Miss Martin — Ruby Martin, I learned much later. As a second grader I don't think I realized that teachers had first names. We didn't really view them as regular people, they were more than that, almost like movie stars or, at least, local celebrities.

Our first grade teacher had been Miss Gladys. Her last name also was Martin, so to avoid confusion she was known to her classes as Miss Gladys, while the second grade teacher was Miss Martin.

Miss Martin was a small woman with gray hair done up in a bun. She was everything a teacher should be — kind, interested, encouraging, stern when necessary — and she looked the part. If I had to cast someone to play a teacher in a play or movie, I would want them to look like Miss Martin.

Anyway, one year Miss Martin decided to initiate a new event. She announced that every Tuesday when we came in from noon recess any student who wished to do so could sing a song or recite a poem or present a reading. I was thrilled! My secret dreams of show business stardom were about to be fulfilled, my previously hidden musical talent unveiled. Immediately I began to prepare for my performance, eagerly awaiting the arrival of the next Tuesday.

But what song would I sing? I mulled over the many possibilities, and my thoughts were drawn to the tunes I had learned in the glow of the little dial on the radio when my brother, Bob, and I listened to broadcasts of The Grand Ol' Opry at night before we fell asleep in the upstairs bedroom of what came to be known as "the house that burned."

Tuesday finally arrived. Morning classes seemed to drag by without end; noon recess, which usually seemed so brief, now was interminable. But finally the big moment came, and when Miss Martin asked if anyone had something to offer, I raised my hand and marched to the front of the room. Taking a deep breath, I launched into my song — the one song I had chosen from all the thousands of songs I might have sung. It went like this:

My brother Bill has a still on the hill
Where he makes a gallon or two.
The buzzards in the sky
Get so dizzy they can't fly
From the smell of that good ol' mountain dew.

There were several verses telling the story of that hillbilly moonshiner, and I sang them all with assured, reedy, and somewhat nasal abandon. When I had finished, there was a moment of silence.

Finally Miss Martin said, "Thank you, Joey. That was very nice." And I returned to my seat.

But my dreams of instant adoration failed to materialize. My classmates did not hoist me onto their shoulders and march around the room, no one asked for my autograph, none of the girls asked me to sit with them on the bus. Nothing changed at all.

The big reception came when I got home.

My sister, Carol Sue, had heard about my performance and, naturally, had to tell my mother. And my poor mother was mortified. What would Miss Martin think? What would all the teachers think? What would our preacher think? Of all the hymns, of all the "nice" popular songs in the world, why *that* song?

I didn't have much to say in my defense, but I knew something my mother didn't. Nothing had changed. Tomorrow I would get on the bus and go to school, and in that warm cocoon of a classroom Miss Martin would introduce us to "The Bears of Blue River," and we would practice our writing and learn to do addition, and I would still be the same old me. Nothing had changed at all.

Printed in the United States
by Baker & Taylor Publisher Services